CW00863766

Beyond the sinking sun

OTENG MONTSHITI

Beyond the sinking sun
Copyright ©2019
CONTACT ADDRESS: OTENG MONTSHITI
P O BOX M1139
KANYE
BOTSWANA

E-MAIL ADDRESS:
otengmontshiti@gmail.com
Contact number: (+267) 74 644 954

Table of contents

Acknowledgements

Writing a book is not an easy task. Therefore I would like to thank our lord Jesus Christ, my family especially my lovely wife who supported.

Chapter 1
Beyond the sinking sun

NOTES

In life challenges will
always be there.
Whether you are a
powerful or weak
person. They will
always come across
your path but what is
of great importance is
how you handle them.

Some people give up
when they come
across their path while
other people are
empowered.

They are not meant to destroy you but to shape your character or life.

Beyond every sinking sun there is a new dawn. New dawn represents new begging's, new thoughts and new strategies. In simple words it means to rewrite the books of your life.

There is no failure under the sun because you can turn your failure into prosperity, stagnation into progress, bareness into fruitfulness and shame into glory. You can turn the circumstances of your life to suit you. Don't give up.

Beyond every sickness there is good health. Beyond every pain there is a gain.

Beyond every storm
there is calmness.
Beyond every mountain
there is a valley. Beyond
every examination there
is a reward.

Beyond every hindrance
there is a breakthrough.
Beyond very struggle
there is freedom.
Beyond every battle
there is victory. It is too
early to give up

We should not give up in life. Keep working harder than never before. Keep on meditating new ideas. That is to say ideas that no one has ever discovered.

Common ideas lead to lack of creativity and uniqueness. Uniqueness of ideas is the only tool which that can give you an up hand when you are with your rivals.

Uniqueness of ideas is the only tools that will make people fail to copy your ideas. You will become versatile. It is not easy to imitate unique people because there discovery is new and very rare.

Common ideas make this world to be stagnated. That is to say run out of ideas. People look the same because they imitate one another.

Do you know why the world is full of wickedness? It is because people like to imitate one another instead of challenging wickedness by their creativity and uniqueness.

The world can't breathe because people don't want to come out of their comfort zone. They want to embrace their weaknesses instead of challenging them. People go to prison so many times because they enjoy that kind of life. People kill because killing is boiling in their blood or they don't want to be life saviors.

People are dying of one and the same disease because they don't want to learn from other people's mistakes.

People don't want to be unique so that they can be remembered by many generations not yet born. Each and everyday we are writing new chapters by what we are doing. What we do today won't end there it will be passed from one generation to another.

Hospitals and prisons are no longer places of rehabilitation because some folks in our society have turned those places into their second home. They don't enjoy anything when they are offered freedom and healing. These places were not created for that.

Imprisonment is when people should reflect back and learn from their past life before they are restored back to their original condition. It is not a place of torture but a moment of being set aside so that you can turn your weakness into strength.

I was shocked one day when a certain brother told me that he missed prison because life was too hard. I looked him into the eyes boldly and said, "You are mad you know how you can enjoy such kind of life like an animal. Do you know that you are an embarrassment to the world?

Today that brother has refrained from that behavior because I did not support his weaknesses. I looked him into the eyes and rebuked him. That is the greatest experience of my life changing people's lives.

Chapter 2
Greatness

NOTES

Greatness is not the accumulation of physical materials but it is when you change people's lives. it is when you share your knowledge and skills to make the world a better place to live in. This world should be the way God has created it to be. Today people say they are great because they are driving nice cars, living big houses and wearing expensive clothes while their fellow brother or sister is sleeping under a bridge or feeding from the dustbins. Greatness is when you look for poor people, widows and widowers, orphans, strangers etc. and share what you have with them.

The world is a dull place because it is all about the survival of the fittest.

This mentality must come to an end because when you are blessed someone is in need of what you are holding. There is nothing like small gift but what matters how you give it. Gift which is offered in front of other people is simply show off. Real giving is done in humility and pure heart.

People die but vision lives on forever.

People who are dreamers keep ideas to themselves and when they die they die with those ideas. But people who are vision holders share what they have (knowledge, skills and ideas) so that they can be celebrated by many generations to come.

People who are great today they sacrificed something to be where they are today.

They have sacrificed their time and other valuable resources to be discovered and be celebrated today. They didn't sit somewhere in a corner and watched a big slice of life passing by. We must be involved in the process of recreating this world to be a better place to live in.

The world is in turmoil men and women of valor must answer the call.

Let us be united to **NOTES** overcome hindrances in this world. We must position ourselves very well and remove wickedness like drug addiction, unfaithfulness, sickness and diseases, jealousy, pride, self centeredness and so forth. We need women and men who will not fear death but know that facing death is part of their assignment on earth.

Greatness is not measured by the number of steps that you take, material wealth and physique but it is measured by the number of challenges you have faced and overcame. Great people never run away from challenges. They celebrate when they come across their path. They celebrate when storms or challenges knocks at the door of their lives they know that an opportunity to grow has finally come.

If you want to know exactly if your friend is great or not ask him or her want he or she wants to do in five years. A weak person would tell you that I want to have a big mall, nice car and so forth but a great person would say I want have big house, family and above all I want to

share what I have with
sick, poor people etc.
That is what
differentiates great
from weak people.
Weak people never
think about anybody
but great people think
about other people's
conditions.

Chapter 3
Leadership

Leadership is the ability to influence other people to achieve a common goal or a specific task.
According to me leadership is not a job it is a calling. In a job set up your primary objective is money but when it comes to the issue of leadership it is all about changing other people's lives.

That is to say it is all about making an impact in the lives of other people in a positive manner.

In simple words leadership is all about putting the interests of other people ahead of yours. You serve other people. In other words you become a servant.

They act of serving other people goes hand in hand with humility. Serving other people without humility is very

destructive because
without it, it is just a
matter of time before
pride knocks at the
door of your heart and
reveals your true colors.

Many people believe
that humility is revealed
when someone is poor
it is not like that. If you
want to test someone's
humility give him
position of influence.
He or she will change
his behavior if that

position goes to his
or head but if he or
she is truly humble he
won't change.

Leadership is not
where you enrich
yourself at the
expense of your
subjects. But it is about
sharing what you have
gathered with them.
Today when people
become powerful they
don't want to associate
themselves with
people

living with disability, widows and widowers etc.

In this world there is one simple rule you are blessed to share whatever you have received with others. It is not wrong to be powerful and successful it only becomes wrong if you don't help or uplift other people.

If we help or uplift other <u>**NOTES**</u> people we add value to life. It becomes colorful or meaningful. True giving is giving what you love the most not what you don't want.

Encourage those who are facing seemingly impossible situations. Bless those who are poor, heal those who are broken hearted and so forth. That is what we

call living a true
legacy behind.

Chapter 4
Mental freedom

There are two types of situations in this world when it comes to the issue of our state of mind. There is what I call mental freedom and imprisonment. Mental imprisonment is when the mind is not creativity. Lack of creativity leads or gives birth to poverty.

When someone is normal, physically fit but he or she is living in the dimension of poverty the root cause is lack of creativity. Dull or idle mind is the soil from which seeds of poverty flourish. Poverty is a mindset because we prosper first in our minds. The powerful discovery today is the end product of a creative mind(s).

If the mind is in bondage that person will only think about rich and famous but

true value of money is
to improve the living
standards of people.
People who are
financially imprisoned
will take other people
and enslave them rather
uplifting them.

People who are
financially imprisoned
will only meditate
prosperity and success
without any
corresponding action. In
simple words their
ideas will suffer pre
mature

death or die without manifesting in the physical world.

They like to blame other people because they don't see anything positive in the lives of other people. If you give them one million dollar they will for your weakness and attack you. They never appreciate anyone in life. They think they are wise while in actual fact they are empty mentally.

On the other hand people who are mentally free always have good ideas. In simple words they are creative. They always come with good ideas to improve the living standards of people. They don't end there they act upon what they meditate about. Meditation without corresponding action is waste of time.

They celebrate when other

people prosper. They make sure they help them. That is to say they don't hesitate to wherever their help is need.

They freely give without any struggle because they know that giving is an investment in eternity. Giving is a seed that will manifest at the rightful time and season. It leads to multiplication and fulfillment in life.

Chapter 5
Seeds

NOTES

Seed is what every one of us is carrying inside. It is called gift or talent. We were given seeds to change the world to be a better place. They multiply when you put them to work.

They can be dormant. In other words they are not functional. They become dormant when someone has not yet discovered his mandate on earth.

In life we can't conquer situations alone. That is why it is important to look for someone who will help you to discover who you are or your purpose. Everybody needs a person to introduce them to new chapters in life. For example, if it is time to prosper financially God will connect you with the rightful people.

People who are facing difficulties

in life the root cause is
that they don't want to
be taught. Education is
the best gift any one
can give you. It leads
to powerful decision
making. Powerful
decision making leads
to robust economy.
Let's face reality if a
country is facing hyper
inflation the root cause
is poor decision
making.

The seed that you are
carrying is

the only tool you can use to move mountains or life challenges. The more you climb mountains the more your seed develops resistance or becomes stronger. A strong seed give birth to a healthy plant and that plant will give birth to healthy fruits.

The word is waiting for the children of man to be revealed to make it a better place.

To bring conciliation where there is friction. It is in pain waiting for the rightful people to comfort it. It is in shame waiting for someone to cover it with glory. It is in despair waiting for someone to give it hope. The big question is that are you that person?

If you are that person what are you waiting for? If you delay your assignment you may start when it is too late. The dangerous part of it is that every man has a replacement if he rejects his or her assignment. Late coming is the author of pains and regrets start now. The calling of your life is now.

Chapter 6
Time

NOTES

Time is a very important **NOTES** factor of life. It is a tool that separates foolish and wise people. It separates successful from poor people. Successful people spend their time investing wisely while poor people waste their valuable time by complaining.

It is used is used to separates chaff from wheat. Chaff is something that is not useful or pure while wheat is useful and pure.

Chaff represents people who spend too much time looking at other people's life. They don't do anything productive. They enjoy useless talks. They spend most of the time under a mango trees and expect miracles to fall on their laps.

But that is not how life was programmed.

Every man eats the fruits **<u>NOTES</u>** of his labor. In simple words, No hard work no success. If you are not a handworker you will not do the will of God in this world because it demands hard working (Genesis 1).

When it comes to the issue of time management God is an expert because he created every in six days and rested on the seventh day.

You see how rest is important? Today people work twenty four hours none stop and expect to be productive. Productivity simply means producing the desired results. If you don't rest your body and mind will be overworked. This can lead sickness or untimely death. In other words you will even lose focus.

While a wheat represents people

who use their time wisely. They prioritize in life. They work in an orderly manner. They are focused and know what they are doing. They don't have divided focus.

They don't give up in life rather they keep on trying until the desired results are produced. They know that persistence pays.

Chapter 7
History

NOTES

History is a very important aspect of our lives. It influences our current situation. If you don't know your past you can't know your future.

You can't solve any problem without knowing its history. That's why doctors and nurses usually ask patients if there are or were people who suffered a certain disease in their family because life is generational.

Some of the problems we are facing today as human being are the results of the decisions that were taken by our forefathers. Some people are going through poverty because their forefathers failed to invest wisely. For example, Jesus Christ died on the cross for us to enjoy the blessings of salvation(wise decision).

If you invest wisely today your children not yet born won't suffer because they will find something to start life with. Wise people prepare for the education of their children before they are born. For example, they buy education policy for them when they are still in their mother's womb.

Don't say my children will bury me bury yourself while you are still alive by buying death insurance cover. Don't say my children will build a nice house for you when they are fully grown up build it yourself. Don't say my children will buy me cars buy it yourself. That mentality is what is delaying the progress of your children.

Your history doesn't determine your future. You can only use historic events to turn your weakness into strength. You should use your past life to motivate and strengthen you in life.

The only problem the world is facing is that people use their past experience as their dwelling place.

They don't want to refrain from their past behavior. Your past life can either be your learning curve or your point of destruction in your life. We should bury the past and move on with our lives.

Do you know why a car has a big window in front and a small window at the back? It is because your past life is not important in your life.

You can't build your future using past records. What is important is the bright future ahead of you. Your focus must be in your future not past life.

Do you know the purpose of rear and side mirrors? It simply means that you should only look at your past life to make sure you don't repeat the same mistakes.

You should only use your past life when you are testifying to someone not make your testimony believable while still keeping your focus in to the future or the road. If you look back you will crash. In simple words dwelling in the past is very destructive.

Chapter 8
Don't try to please people

NOTES

In life be yourself.
Don't try to be
something you are not
just because you want
to be accommodated
and appreciated by
other people. People
should love you the
way you are. We are
not saying support
your weakness but be
the real you.

Pretending to be
something you are not
is extremely dangerous
because

when situations come or knock at the door of your life you will be revealed.

When people are not treating you in the rightful way don't keep quite because you want to be known as a saint. Nobody will come from somewhere and fight your battles. Just look them into the eyes and say, "That is not the way I want to be treated. Treat me the way you want to be treated in life." That is the golden rule of life.

You are not a door mat. You are a dignified human being. You deserve better treatment in life. Don't let people abuse you and keep silent. Doesn't whisper in the deep you should speak out.

That is good at all. People should know

what you want and
what you don't want in
life. It is better to be
alone rather than to be
treated inhumanly. You
must set boundaries in
your life. Life without
principles is life
without value.

Today people don't
tolerate other people's
religion or faith
because they lack the
spirit of appreciating
people the way they
are.

Don't try to change people love them the way they are. Above all their right of worship is enforced by constitution of every country that embraces the principles of democracy all over the world.

Do you know why nations, brothers and sisters fight one another? The root cause is that we want to change people instead of loving them the way they are. The

moment you want to change people the way they are and be what you want be ready for a long life battle with every one you meet across your path.

God didn't wait for us to change before he released Jesus Christ to die for our sins. He released him with unconditional love. That is what is called agape love or God kind of love (1 Corinthians 13 and John 3:16). The problem is that we relate with other people based on conditions and anything based on condition won't pass the test of time. Unconditional love is the key to a better world.

Chapter 9
Dig deeper inside of you

NOTES

Life is not for the faint hearted it is for those people who fight for what they want. Nothing in this world comes without struggle therefore life is a battle ground.

Everyday we are engaged in a war in one way or another. Some people are battling to get out of poverty while someone somewhere is fighting criminal cases in the court of law. Life is a battle field indeed.

People who survive in this world are those who have purposed their hearts or made decision to never give up in life. They never permit their current situations to determine the way they view life. If they are struggling to get out of poverty they fill their minds with positive ideas. If someone gives up easily the root cause is weak mindset. Strong mindset prevails during trying times.

During hard times dig deeper than never before and discover what is inside of you. That is the seed or talent that you need to make the world a better place.

Some people use their talent of writing like me to make the world a better place to live in while other people use their speaking abilities to speak comfort, encouragement and correction in the lives of other people. In simple words we are gifted differently to change people's lives differently.

Therefore, there is no need for us to be engaged in

unhealthy competition. We should be content with what God has given us.

Some people fast and pray to cultivate what is inside of them. Do whatever it takes to reach your true potential but never give up. Life will always give the opposite of what you want or desire until you get out of the comfort zone and fight like never before.

Don't ever think people who are successful today it was easy. They went through a lot before they are celebrated. Hard work and success go together. They are twins. You can't separate the two.

One of my successful friend told me that he used to eat soft porridge before success comes and knocks at the door of his life.

Doors of prosperity were opened every where.

So don't be interested in the end results rather be interested in the processes of success. Learn from successful persons how they managed to be where they are today.

Chapter 10
Don't expect quick results

NOTES

In life success is a
process. It takes time. So
build your life one step
at a time. Success is
simply small successful
steps taken over a long
period of time. Quick
success is very
dangerous you will end
up taking things you
don't know where they
come from.

Everything done in a
hurry loses quality or is
very destructive. Just
relax and do your things
slowly.

Even powerful authors today started somewhere small and grew with time. They started by making sure they write what people what and produced quality materials. That is what is called brand creation in marketing.

Powerful brands today went through a lot before they are known today. It is simply keeping your promises that bring credibility.

Credibility is a
process also.

Chapter 11
Never stop learning

NOTES

In life knowledge is power so it is wrong to stop learning. The more you learn the more you are empowered. Empowered mind leads to quality decision making and quality decision making leads to the kind of life you desire.

Never stop reading books, watching tapes and videos which are informative because the more you listen or read them is the more your mind is reprogrammed.

Learning is not easy it requires a teachable heart. A teachable heart is ready to be taught, corrected and be encouraged. It requires total humility to learn. It means submit to someone and it is not easy.

People who are learned today they were taught by someone because people are born without knowing anything. Learning is life long life process. If you stop learning your mental development will decline. You must read atleast two books monthly because knowledge is the food of the brain.

Idle mind is the breeding ground of negative thoughts. Don't stay alone for too long without engaging your mind. If you are bored of reading books visit friends who motivate you to work hard in life not those friends who support your weakness.

You should keep friends who are handworkers and

successful in life in
your inner cycle. Don't
keep people who exalt
you when you not
creative. Keep people
who will challenge
your creativity.

The best gift anyone
can give you is to
teach you how to
become successful in
life. Don't listen to
good part of the
teachings bad
experiences are also
important.

The problem with us is
that we like to listen to
sweet stories but it
won't teach you the
true reality of life. Life
is a mixture of bad
and good times. When
you combine the two
they give you true
meaning of life.

If the story is all about
good things it is just a
fairy tale. It can't
change anyone the
way they view life.

In life there are many mountains to climb and many rivers to swim.it is not a smooth road i.e. it is bumpy before you can enjoy freedom, wealth, peace of mind and so forth.

If you want to be on top of the world be ready for big and unusual challenges because unique people overcome unique situations. They are just there to speak strength to you. Never give up.

Lightning Source UK Ltd.
Milton Keynes UK
UKHW050304280222
399263UK00015B/270